Bowl the Maidens Over
Our First Women Cricketers

Bowl the Maidens Over: Our First Women Cricketers

LZS Press

www.LZSPress.com.au

First published in 2019 *The Yorker*, MCC Library, Melbourne
Revised and expanded edition published 2021 by LZS Press
Reprinted in 2021

Copyright text © Louise Zedda-Sampson
www.LZSPress.com.au

Quotations from newspaper articles have been reproduced as they appear in the original source, retaining original spelling, grammar and punctuation unless otherwise indicated.

ISBN: 978-0-6451255-1-1 (paperback)
ISBN: 978-0-6451255-0-4 (hardback)

A catalogue record for this book is available from the National Library of Australia

All rights reserved. No part of this publication may be reproduced in whole or in part, stored in a retrievable system, or transmitted in any form or by any means, electronic, mechanical, photocopying, recording or otherwise, without written permission of the copyright holder or publisher.

Cover illustrations: British Newspaper Archive: 1888, 'Harrow vs Pinner', *The Graphic*, 18 August, viewed 19 February 2021, https://blog.britishnewspaperarchive.co.uk/2019/07/16/july-2019-early-history-of-womens-cricket/

Design: Lorna Hendry

BOWL THE MAIDENS OVER

OUR FIRST WOMEN CRICKETERS

LOUISE ZEDDA-SAMPSON

FOREWORD

Women are largely absent in the annals of sporting history as participants or commentators – traditionally they have been relegated to silent and passive roles conforming to a prescribed female stereotype. It's so refreshing that change is afoot, and that stories of women in sport written by women are now being published.

It's especially delightful to stumble across a forgotten cricket story that has inexplicably been overlooked. Louise Zedda-Sampson provides us with just that. *Bowl the Maidens Over* sympathetically and comprehensively recounts the story of early women's cricket, detailing the challenges faced by playing a man's game.

The first women's charity match took place on 7 April 1874 and was met by extensive press vitriol and public scorn. The encounter was deemed so audacious that newspaper reports of the match even reached English and American shores. Notwithstanding vehement criticism, the women's enthusiasm remained buoyant and subsequent encounters were arranged. Despite fits and starts, this marks the birth of the women's competition. Parallels between the early days of women's cricket and the emergence of the women's AFL competition are drawn and made all the more pertinent by the familial linkage of key personnel of both the competitions separated by over a century. This publication celebrates women's cricket and the pioneering women involved. It resonates across the spheres of sport, culture, history and feminism – functioning as a barometer which informs wider ideological sentiments of the day.

From its humble beginnings, the women's game has grown over the past century and a half. The contemporary competition would be barely recognised by the cricketers at Camp Reserve. Women's cricket today is immensely popular, as evidenced by the record crowd of 86,174 who attended the World Cup final at the Melbourne Cricket Club in 2020 on International Women's Day. A cameo performance by music superstar Katy Perry added to the excitement. It was a day to be celebrated as was the match on 7 April 1874, which should be viewed as the harbinger of the contemporary game.

Dr Megan Ponsford

CONTENTS

Acknowledgements 1

Where it all began 5
Preparing for the match 7
The first innings for women's cricket 13
Post-match fallout 25
Off the field 45
Women's rights and men's wrongs 46
A second innings for Sandhurst 51
Post-match wind-up 59
All out 67
The maidens over 71

Figures 81
Endnotes 84

ACKNOWLEDGEMENTS

Thanks first to my family who lose me every time I get lost in the past. Special thanks to my husband, Paul, who, with my supportive writer friends, especially Rebecca Fraser and Kathryn Hore, knew I could do this book before I did.

A shout-out to the Youlden Parkville Cricket Club because in researching the records for your club history as a student volunteer, I found this story.

Thanks to Trevor Ruddell at the Melbourne Cricket Club Library for first publishing this story and sharing my enthusiasm for the topic. Thanks also to Lorna Hendry and the editors and proofreaders who have assisted with the production of this book.

And the biggest thanks of all goes to the brave women cricketers in this book and their supporters who have helped pave a way for other women to play competitive sports.

FIGURE 1 Rae's Ironbark School staff photo.
Photo: N. J. Claire courtesy S. G. Rae, *The Age*, 1936.

Fom left to right:

FRONT ROW: Misses Chambers (afterwards Lady Murdoch, aunt of the eminent pianist, William Murdoch), Sheldon, Williams, Mrs. John Rae, the head teacher, Misses Barbara Rae, Mungovan. Fosdyke, Nellie Rae, Susannah Evans.

BACK ROW: John Rae, jun, William Rae, Robert Craig, Alex, Rae, Sam Bolitho.

IN THE BACKGROUND: Jim Smith.

This photograph was taken about 1877.

For fame or thanks we came not here;
But now a cause we all revere
Calls out to us for aid.

While fathers on a sick bed lie,
To win the bread poor mothers try;
But children hungry round them cry—
And for their sakes we played.

Not for the game itself we care,
Some bumps and jeers we had to dare;
Yet Charity with pleading prayer,
Urged not her claim in vain.

Your thanks we kindly take;
And when an effort next you make
For Charity the Angel's sake,
We'll do our best again.

BARBARA RAE, 1874

FIGURE 2 Men playing cricket, women croquet.
The Australian News for Home Readers, 24 December 1864.

WHERE IT ALL BEGAN

Today, competitive cricket is played by women and men alike. People assume that this is only a recent change – perhaps within the last few years. But is this really the case? When we look through the pages of Australia's past, we can see that women's sports have been played competitively in Australia intermittently for almost 150 years, and that it wasn't only croquet that was played by the Victorian ladies of the 1800s.

So, why does it seem like women's competitive cricket is a recent development when women's cricket history has such a rich and colourful past? It could be said that the weight of oppression was too strong and that women couldn't or wouldn't play, but it's simply not true. Women have always wanted to play and when given the opportunity, have demonstrated they are skilled, capable and willing.

The answer to why women's participation in cricket in Australia was interrupted at its peak may lie in the attitudes and responses to these earlier events. Early women cricketers were accused of being unladylike and unfeminine, or their play was sexualised, their sporting displays likened to burlesque shows. A cricketer's character and physique were brought into question more frequently than her ability to play. Such attitudes have

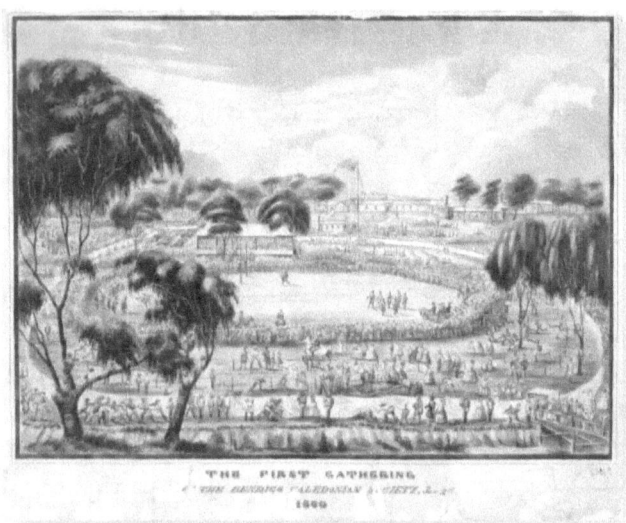

FIGURE 3 Sketch of Camp Reserve.
The First Gathering of the Bendigo Caledonian Society, Jan. 2nd, 1860, George Lacy, National Library of Australia, 1860.

persisted to current day, but thankfully we are stepping out of this period of subjugation and women have more opportunities to play the sports they love.

This book examines the achievements of women cricketers through newspaper reports of the day. We start this journey by visiting 1874 and the first women's cricket match played at the Camp Reserve (Figure 3) at the Sandhurst Easter Fair.

PREPARING FOR THE MATCH

The first organised, revenue-raising, spectator match of Australian women's cricket was played in Sandhurst (now known as Bendigo) in 1874. It was a charity match held during the fourth Sandhurst Easter Fair with a spectator entrance fee intended to raise funds for the Bendigo Hospital and Benevolent Asylum. The women cricketers were practised, professional and played in front of a male and female crowd, with some people travelling considerable distances to attend the event.

This first match was organised by John Rae, the headmaster of Ironbark School. There were two teams of eleven: the Reds, captained by Rae's wife, Mrs Emily Rae, who was also Ironbark's head teacher, and the Blues, captained by their daughter, Barbara Rae. Another of the Raes' daughters also played in this match: Helen, who was known affectionately as Nellie. Both daughters were also schoolteachers.

GRAND EASTER FAIR.

FOURTH ANNIVERSARY
IN AID OF THE
BENDIGO HOSPITAL
AND
BENEVOLENT ASYLUM.

THE Committee—consisting of Delegates from the Hospital, Benevolent Asylum, and Benefit Societies—will hold their

FOURTH GRAND EASTER FAIR,
ON
MONDAY & TUESDAY,

THE 6TH AND 7TH OF APRIL,

In aid of the above most deserving Charitable Institutions, in that magnificent Park, known as the

CAMP RESERVE,

The Committee intend to hold

A GRAND FAIR

For the disposition by Sale,
or otherwise, of such articles as may be contributed
by the charitable.
EVERY DESCRIPTION OF AMUSEMENT.
SPORTS,
THEATRICAL—MUSIC (INSTRUMENTAL and
VOCAL)—WAXWORKS—DANCING,
BOATING,
GRAND BABY SHOW,

In fact everything obtainable and available as a
source of pleasure and amusement will be
provided.

FIGURE 4 Easter Fair advertisement. *Bendigo Advertiser*, 5 March 1874.

Tracking the advertisements in the *Bendigo Advertiser*, the first notice for the fourth anniversary 'Grand Easter Fair' appeared on 5 March 1874 (Figure 4). Another notice followed on 13 March, this time seeking 'performers and amusements' (Figure 5). Shortly after that, on 17 March, appeared the first Australian advertisement calling for women cricketers, alongside a call for women to collect money on behalf of the Easter Fair (Figure 6).

Two days after this notice was published, a further notice announced that Barbara Rae had obtained permission from the Bendigo United Cricket Club (BUCC) to use the Back Creek Cricket Ground and club equipment for practice.[1]

The women were taking this game seriously. Using the BUCC grounds and equipment to train, they were no doubt coached by the BUCC men who were some of the finest cricketers in Victoria. Several BUCC cricketers had gained national attention in December 1873 as part of the Victorian team that defeated a visiting all-English team for the first time in Australian history.

Over the next week or so Barbara Rae's advertisements calling for 'ladies who are desirous of playing', continued to appear in the *Bendigo Advertiser*. There were thirty to forty applications and two teams of eleven were easily formed. The news that a ladies' cricket match was to be played at a regional Victorian country town was reported in several states and many city and district newspapers spread across Australia. It was newsworthy in Tasmania's *The Cornwall Chronical*, and as

NOTICE.

FOURTH GRAND ANNUAL EASTER FAIR,
Camp Reserve, Sandhurst.

ALL Persons who are Proprietors or Lessees of any kind of Amusements, say, Japanese jugglers, acrobats, hippodromes, Richardson's or any other theatrical shows, Aunt Sally, shooting galleries, merry-go-rounds, &c., &c., are invited to forward applications, stating amount offered for such portions as required for the enclosed ground. Applications to be sent in not later than Wednesday, 18th March, at four p.m.

ROBERT DENYER, Secretary
Office—Camp Reserve. 3331

FIGURE 5 Advertisement.
Bendigo Advertiser, 13 March 1874.

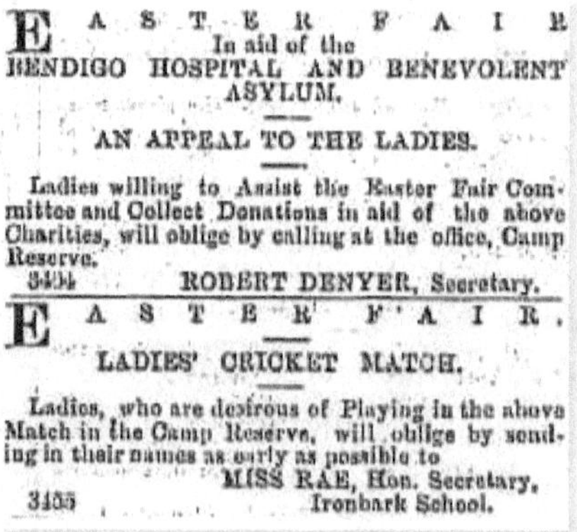

EASTER FAIR
In aid of the
BENDIGO HOSPITAL AND BENEVOLENT ASYLUM.

AN APPEAL TO THE LADIES.

Ladies willing to Assist the Easter Fair Committee and Collect Donations in aid of the above Charities, will oblige by calling at the office, Camp Reserve.
3434   ROBERT DENYER, Secretary.

EASTER FAIR.

LADIES' CRICKET MATCH.

Ladies, who are desirous of Playing in the above Match in the Camp Reserve, will oblige by sending in their names as early as possible to
MISS RAE, Hon. Secretary,
3435   Ironbark School.

FIGURE 6 Advertisements.
Bendigo Advertiser, 17 March 1874.

far away as Queensland in the *Gympie Times and Mary River Mining Gazette*.[2]

One report stated the ladies would play in a bloomer costume (Figure 7). The suggestion that the team would favour this attire over the usual neck-to-toe dresses worn by ladies at all times brought society to a standstill. Barbara Rae quickly notified the *Bendigo Advertiser* on 26 March that this would not be the case, then followed up with a report in the *Bendigo Evening Star*, clarifying the matter and calming the furore (Figure 8 and 9). This is also an interesting example as it shows how the ladies' appearance was deemed more newsworthy than their sporting abilities.

The comments also showed the women's approach to the match was logical, well-considered and professional, a clear display of their seriousness and commitment to the sport.

The *Melbourne Punch* from 26 March conveyed great excitement about the match, even though the comments were geared more towards the ladies' looks than their skill (Figure 10).

The Sandhurst Easter Fair was advertised as a two-day fair. It would start, as customary, with a parade through the Sandhurst streets showcasing performers, contributors, dignitaries, and this year, the women cricketers.

On the morning of the match, the weather was overcast and threatening but nothing was going to spoil the women cricketers' proud moment. The skies cleared to a brilliant blue just in time for the parade. The cricketers wore custom-made uniforms of white calico dresses

FIGURE 7 Mrs Amelia Bloomer wearing the bloomer costume. *The Pictorial Australian*, 1895.

with pink or blue jackets, the jacket colour representing the respective team. Even though the jackets were pink and of the 'zouave' (Figure 11) style, the media reported the style as 'garibaldi' (Figure 12) and the colour of the pink jackets and team as red.

There was a great deal of local support and enthusiasm, with many people in the crowd drawn to see the debuting women cricketers. The crowds consisted of people from all over Victoria. *The Argus* stated that trains brought visitors from Melbourne and Echuca, and due to excessive numbers, several hundred people had to be left behind at Castlemaine.[3] It was estimated 20,000 people attended this first day of the fair.

THE FIRST INNINGS FOR WOMEN'S CRICKET

The pre-match excitement was palpable. No one had seen a match like this before. Novelty cricket matches had been held by theatre companies in the past but they were comical performances rather than actual matches.[4] Women's cricket was a matter of great interest, so much so, the Star Comique Company announced that on the evening of the match a bat would be awarded to the highest scorer.[5]

On the day of the match, 7 April, the match was even listed first in the *Bendigo Advertiser* in the day's events, pushing the fire brigade and fireworks – historically the main features of the fair – to second spot (Figure 13).

LADIES' CRICKET MATCH.—We are requested by the honorary secretary of the ladies' cricket match to correct a mistake which has been made with regard to the costume in which they are to appear in the field. The "Bloomer costume" was never thought of. The dresses are to be made by Messrs. Buick and Co., of white calico, the full length, the distinguishing badge being a Zouave jacket of pink for one side, and blue for the other.

FIGURE 8 Correction regarding the bloomer costume. *Bendigo Advertiser*, 26 March 1874.

Referring to the ladies' cricket match, which is to be played at Sandhurst during the Easter Fair, the *Bendigo Evening Star* writes:—"How to give due effect to dress in a theatre so strange and novel as the green sward of the cricket ground, has lately exercised the minds of our ladies. Certainly, considering the nature of the game, with its leg-byes, and so forth, the Bloomer costume might be deemed the most convenient and appropriate for the evolutions of the field. But we quite approve of the resolution of the ladies who are strong-minded enough to appear publicly in a game that is essentially masculine, to show still further their strength of mind in determining to play it out in 'long clothes,' rather than à la Bloomer. So it has been proposed, seconded, and duly carried by the lady players, that they will make their appearance in the field in calico dresses 'of the full length;' the calico on both sides being white, and the distinguishing badges being zouave jackets of pink and blue respectively."

FIGURE 9 Further correction regarding the bloomer costume. *The Ballarat Courier*, 28 March 1874.

At noon, as the fair opened for the second day, the cricketers arrived at the cricket ground in the same three carriages they had ridden in as part of the parade. Spectators numbered in the thousands. Mrs Rae led the Reds, and Barbara Rae, the Blues from the tent: two by two, arms linked – one pink one blue – backs straight, heads held high. They were greeted with loud applause. The women assembled on the ground in their teams: their ability for organisation further impressing the crowd.

A report by the *Bendigo Advertiser* on 8 April best covers the entire match and offers a clear sense of pride in the players.[6]

THE LADIES' CRICKET MATCH.
Bendigo Advertiser, 8 April 1874

It certainly required a very considerable amount of courage on the part of the ladies to undertake to play a cricket match in public. The thing was unprecedented as far as Australia was concerned, and such a remarkable event as a ladies' cricket match has seldom happened, even in the old country— the home of cricket. The cause in which they were engaged however—that of "heavenborn charity"—over-came all scruples, and they came nobly forward to aid the destitute and the suffering.

Sandhurst has the honor of turning out the first twenty-two lady cricketers, and from the

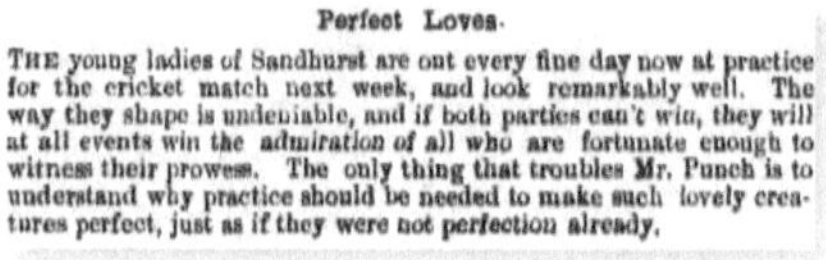

Perfect Loves.

THE young ladies of Sandhurst are out every fine day now at practice for the cricket match next week, and look remarkably well. The way they shape is undeniable, and if both parties can't win, they will at all events win the *admiration of all* who are fortunate enough to witness their prowess. The only thing that troubles Mr. Punch is to understand why practice should be needed to make such lovely creatures perfect, just as if they were not *perfection* already.

FIGURE 10 The ladies at cricket practice. *Melbourne Punch*, 26 March 1874.

FIGURE 11 Zouave jackets illustration. *Godey's Magazine*. *v.64*, 1862 Jan–Jun.

exhibition of their capabilities yesterday in this new field of love's labor they have added an additional charm to the game of cricket, and shown that, as a healthy exercise, it is alike fitted for the gentler as for the sterner sex. The match was originated in aid of the funds of the hospital and asylum, and the large crowd of spectators who gathered yesterday to witness it evinced an amount of public interest in it far beyond what was expected.

For some weeks past the ladies had been practising the game on the Back Creek Cricket Ground, kindly placed at their disposal by the B.U.C.C., and the progress which they made was astonishing, for they picked up the points of the game with wonderful aptitude. At first it was expected that they should play in the Bloomer costume, as being less likely to interfere with their freedom of movement than any other, but the innovation was considered too startling for a British community, and the idea was given up in favour of an attire of the ordinary shaped dress, made of calico, with a colored jacket to distinguish the respective sides. These dresses the ladies purpose handing over as gifts to the charities. The game was intended to be played on the Back Creek Cricket ground, but unforeseen circumstances prevented it taking place there, and it was played in the Camp Reserve.

FIGURE 12 Garibaldi shirt illustration. *Godey's Magazine. v.64*, 1862 Jan–Jun.

At one o'clock the ladies, in full costume, arrived in three carriages. The wickets were pitched in one of the crosswalks by the umpires—Mr. J. Latham and Mr. John Glen who officiated in the absence of the Hon. A. Mackay. Everything being in readiness, the ladies—the one side wearing red Garibaldi jackets and sailors' hats; and the other blue jackets and similar hats—marched in pairs—red and blue being linked together—from the tent into the field, headed by respective captains—Mrs. Rae for the Reds, and Miss B. Rae for the Blues.

Their appearance was very pretty and picturesque; and they were loudly applauded by the onlookers. It was suddenly discovered that though the ladies had brought bats and wickets, they had forgotten the ball, but this little difficulty was got over by one of the umpires producing one of Duke's best. The respective captains having tossed for innings it was decided that the Reds should go to the bat and they secured a total of 62 runs before the last wicket fell.

The highest scorer was Miss Kate Petrie who obtained 27 runs. This young lady not only acquitted herself well with the bat, but she trundled the ball with effect. Miss Nellie Rae distinguished herself by smart fielding, effecting a capital catch by which a good bat, Miss Clay, was got rid of. Miss J. Murdoch

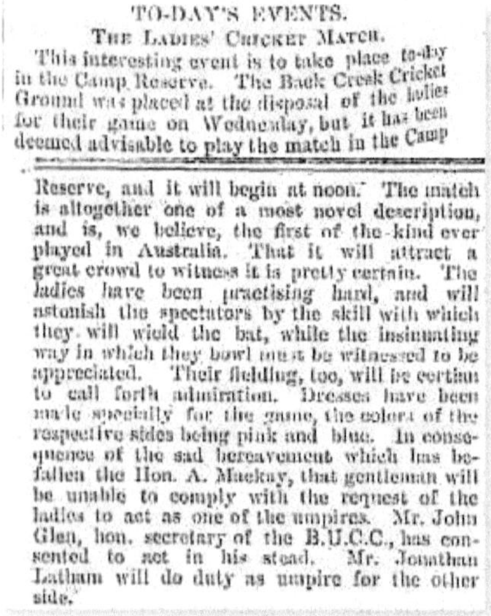

TO-DAY'S EVENTS.

THE LADIES' CRICKET MATCH.

This interesting event is to take place to-day in the Camp Reserve. The Back Creek Cricket Ground was placed at the disposal of the ladies for their game on Wednesday, but it has been deemed advisable to play the match in the Camp Reserve, and it will begin at noon. The match is altogether one of a most novel description, and is, we believe, the first of the kind ever played in Australia. That it will attract a great crowd to witness it is pretty certain. The ladies have been practising hard, and will astonish the spectators by the skill with which they will wield the bat, while the insinuating way in which they bowl must be witnessed to be appreciated. Their fielding, too, will be certain to call forth admiration. Dresses have been made specially for the game, the colors of the respective sides being pink and blue. In consequence of the sad bereavement which has befallen the Hon. A. Mackay, that gentleman will be unable to comply with the request of the ladies to act as one of the umpires. Mr. John Glen, hon. secretary of the B.U.C.C, has consented to act in his stead. Mr. Jonathan Latham will do duty as umpire for the other side.

FIGURE 13 Anticipation grows for the ladies' cricket match. *Bendigo Advertiser*, 7 April 1874.

proved herself a first rate bowler. After the lapse of half an hour the Reds took the field, and they put their opponents out for 83 runs. Miss B. Rae was top scorer, with 36 not out; while Miss Gerber scored 10; and besides did good execution with the ball, bowling underhand with precision, and lowering six wickets. Miss Clay caught out Miss Luthwhyte by a splendid left-hand catch, which evoked tremendous applause, and brought the innings to a close.

One innings each only was played, and victory therefore rested with the Blues. Mr. Coffin acted as scorer. When the ladies had assembled in the booth Mr. Abbott, chairman of the hospital committee, thanked the ladies for the successful effort which they had made on behalf of the charities, and the gentlemen present sang "They are jolly good fellows." Mrs. Rae, on behalf of the ladies, replied, stating that the ladies had thoroughly enjoyed the game, and had the utmost gratification in knowing that their efforts had been productive of a substantial addition to the funds of the charities.

Annexed is the score:—

THE REDS.
Mrs. Rae (capt.), b Gerber. 4
Miss K.Petrie, run out 27
Miss N. Rae, b Gerber 6
Miss J. Murdoch, b Gerber 7

Miss L. Williams, b Gerber 5
Miss E. Carr, b B. Rae 1
Mrs Hoffner, b Gerber 3
Miss A. Williams, run out 2
Mrs. Leeds, not out 4
Miss R. Shalders, b Gerber 1
Miss Luthwhyte, c Clay, b Gerber 0
No ball, 1; bye, 1 2
Total 62

THE BLUES.
Miss Richardson, b K. Petrie 2
Miss Carpenter, b K. Petrie 6
Miss C. Shalders, b K. Petrie 1
Miss Clay, c N. Rae, b K. Petrie 0
Miss A. Petrie, b Murdoch 1
Miss B. Rae (cap.), not out 36
Miss E. Gerber, c K. Petrie, b N. Rae 10
Miss Wiseman, b K. Petrie 6
Miss Westhead, h w, b Mrs. Rae 8
Miss M. Bell, b J. Murdoch 8
Mrs. Drought, b J. Murdoch 0
Byes 3, wides 2 5
Total 83

A separate article appeared in the *Bendigo Advertiser* on the same day titled 'Second Day', with the commentary focused on the crowd, the increase in female attendance and the fact that all spectators were totally captivated by the cricket.[7]

THE EASTER FAIR.
SECOND DAY. *(extract)*
Bendigo Advertiser, 8 April 1874

In the afternoon all who were able to do so witnessed the novelty taking the form of a ladies' cricket match. This match was undoubtedly the chief attraction of the day and was watched during the progress of the play with the greatest of interest.

There was a large sprinkling of the fair sex, who, in proportion, mustered in greater force than on the first day of the fair. Many of them were doubtless drawn from home by the novelty of seeing some of their own sex playing at the "manly game" of cricket, to see what figure they would present, or for a number of other reasons which it would be needless to include in our remarks. However, their presence was most welcome, as it ever is, and imparted a brilliancy to the scene which was absent on the first day of the fair.

The ladies' cricket match was commenced shortly after twelve o'clock, at which time the fair was duly opened, but the booths, etc., were neglected for the time and the attention of all the visitors was centred on the sight of the day.

CONTENTS OF TO-DAY'S PAPER.

INDEX TO NEWS.

	Page
A Defaulting Bank Manager	9
Ballarat	5
Borough Councils	10
Charge of Manslaughter Against a Nurse	9
Commercial	6
Congregational Union and Mission of Victoria	5
Correspondence—	
The Tariff—Its Effects on Intercolonial Trade	9
Country News	10
Cricket—	
East Melbourne v. Fifteen of Ovens District	9
The Ladies' Cricket Match at Sandhurst	9
Elections—Mr. Francis at Richmond	8
Geelong Wool and Station Produce Report	11
Inquests	10
Law Report	10
Leaders, Sub-Leaders, Town News, Telegrams, &c.	6-7
Marquis of Lorne Case	9
Melbourne Markets	11
Melbourne Wool and Station Produce Report	11
Mining Notes	11
News by the Mail—	
Our Paris Letter	4
Germany	4
The Duchess of Edinburgh	4
The Latin Aspect of the New Church Struggle	4-5
New South Wales	5
New Mission Schooner Southern Cross	10
Opera	5
P. and O. Service	9
Police	10
Shipping	6
Shire Councils	10
South Australia	5
Terrible Lamp Explosion	5
Town Council—Fitzroy	10
Volunteers	10

FIGURE 14 The ladies' match appears with the East Melbourne Cricket Club match.
The Argus, 9 April 1874.

The above observation was reinforced by a report in the finance pages of *The Argus* also on 8 April. When the report referred to stocks and trading in Sandhurst for the day of the match, it was noted:[8]

> **COMMERCIAL INTELLIGENCE.**
> *(extract)*
> *The Argus,* 8 April 1874
>
> There was some slight effort made to do business this morning, but it soon became evident that the few people present were not in the vein, the attraction of a ladies' cricket match at the Easter fair being too much even for the most determined and persevering brokers.

POST-MATCH FALLOUT

In *The Argus* on 9 April, two days after the match, the women shared a spot in the index under the heading 'Cricket', appearing next to the well-established and prominent East Melbourne Cricket Club. It was completely unheard of in the day to have women's sporting results appear in such a publication, let alone appear next to the men's results (Figure 14).

But all the goodwill dissipated practically overnight. Maybe the equality of appearing next to the men's results was one of the things that set the critics off. Another contributing factor may have been the alleged catcalling and heckling at the match. Reports had surfaced in several newspapers of poor behaviour by youth and males jeering the women cricketers.

Even before the fallout from the match had hit the newspapers, the effects were clearly felt by the women. On a day that should have been cause for celebration, there was withdrawal. When the prize bat was scheduled to be presented to Barbara Rae, a letter was read out stating Miss Rae and the other cricketers could not attend as they had decided not to appear in public unless it was for a charitable cause.[9]

The bat had a broad, blue silk ribbon tied around it with the following inscription in gold lettering:

> Bendigo Easter Fair.
> Presented to Miss Barbara Rae, in commemoration of her being the highest scorer at the Ladies' Cricket Match, 1874.

Whatever the real reasons, the women could not celebrate their achievements.

This one cricket match had created a massive gender war. Its target, the women. Although the match had been strongly supported and well-patronised at the time, the fallout was vicious and vindictive.

Two days after the match, on Thursday 9 April, a mocking article appeared in the *Melbourne Punch*.[10] The author ridiculed the cricketers, attributing them names such as Alice Shy, Miss Sharp, Miss Needles, as well as reducing the match to a series of events that involved flying 'hairpins' and 'hair pads' rather than offering any valid commentary.

THE LADIES' CRICKET MATCH.
Melbourne Punch, 9 April 1874

(SUBJOINED is an account of this match from our own reporter, a man on whom we cannot place the slightest reliance. Perhaps under these circumstances the public will be good enough to take it for what it is worth.)

This match came off on Easter Monday in connexion with the Sandhurst fair. (We have cut out all this till we came to the play.) Precisely at 12, Mrs. Rae and Miss Rae skied a coin—"man, lovely man," cried Miss Rae, and man it was. "We go in," said Miss Rae, "and you will be good enough to take the field." After a little time was cut to waste in arguing the point, Mrs. Rae turned out and placed her women thus: Miss A. Bell trundled the leather; Miss W. Jupp kept wicket; Miss A. Wheeler, leg; Miss S. Sharp, short slip; Miss J. Needle, point; Miss H. Grace (a little nugget of a woman), long off; Miss D. Ebsworth, cover point; Mrs. Gamp, mid-on; Mrs E. Sutton, third woman up; Mrs. J. Breakaway, long stop; Mrs. V. Stout, long slip.

All being ready, Miss Rae and Miss Goldsmid quickly took their places at the wicket to the bowling of Miss Bell and Miss Sharp. The first over from Miss Bell was a maiden. Then Miss Goldsmid drove Miss Sharp for a couple. Miss Bell's three next overs were maidens, and in the next from Miss Sharp, Miss Goldsmid tried to stop with her legs. "How's that, umpire?" "Out." And out she went, amidst cries of "poor dear Emily—so unexpected;" "how well she bears up," &c., &c.

Miss Tallboys was the next to handle the willow, and she rattled twenty together in fine style. By this time Miss Rae's time had come, and she was taken by Mrs. Gamp, at mid on. 2—40—20. Miss Moses took Miss Rae's place, and in the first over, put Miss Sharp under her leg for a brace, then poked Mrs. Rae for 4, and in the next over her middle stump was sent flying. 3—46—6. Miss Williams was the next to appear, and was greeted with a round of applause, for she was known to be "a regular wunner" at practice. She was missed at cover point the first over (the fieldswoman not making an effort), and then taken by Miss Sharp in the slips the next. "No great catch you mean thing, Miss Sharp," she said, as she returned with her *retroussé* nose high in the air. 4—46—0.

About this time I got a good deal confused with the heat (which was very oppressive), and the dust which came up in clouds. I took a little brandy to keep my nervous system in order, but it had the contrary effect. The only thing I distinctly remember was that Miss Sharp had sometimes 12 balls to the over, and that one of the ladies bet the other a "brigand hat" that she was not out. I have also a faint recollection of Miss Rae asking the umpire to "put up the needles" meaning the stumps, and of Miss Wheedle's being bowled off her hair pads, and the hair pins flying in all directions. But in spite of these misty recollections it was a most enjoyable day, and—I subjoin the scores—taken from the scoring book, as I fear to trust my notes.

MISS RAE'S SIDE.
Miss Rae, run out... 36
Mrs. Barbara Jones, skirts b.w. 20
Miss E. Philpot, run out (stopping to pick up improver) 14
Miss Jane Sellers, c. and b. Mrs Rae. 0
Miss Helen Spitfire, wouldn't go out 10
Miss Alice Shy, couldn't be persuaded to go in 0
Miss Tallboys, l. b. w.. 40
Miss Goldsmid, pannier before wicket. 8
Miss J. Bell
Miss E. Bell, skirts, legs, and stiff petticoats b.w. 20
Miss O. Bell
Total, more or less. 148

MRS. RAE'S SIDE.
Miss Bell, 1st and 2nd innings (she would not go out) 0
Miss Jupp 10
Miss Wheeler, hit wicket out of spite 20
Miss Sharp, improver before wicket 4
Miss Needle 10
Miss Grace, hair pads 12
Miss Ebsworth b. Miss Rae 10
Mrs. Gamp, run out of breath 0
Mrs. Sutton, c. and b. Miss Rae 0
Mrs. Breakaway, abused out Miss Rae 55
Mrs. Stout, carried out 6
Total 127

The *Melbourne Punch* wasn't the only newspaper to cause problems for the women. Only a few days later, *The Herald* published an article called 'WOMAN!' attacking the cricketers and comparing them to the women suffragettes in Ohio who were 'storming' men's drinking places and ruining all their fun. *The Herald* basically espoused that women caused men to drink and gamble in the first place and that maybe if the women were home more and spent less of their money on things like hats and fashion, men wouldn't need to drink.[11] This extract is the final commentary in the article. It summarises the author's and what appeared at the time to be a great deal of the public's views:

WOMAN! (extract)
The Herald, 11 April 1874

Nay, even as the other day at Sandhurst, she will display her brazen charms in broad daylight to a miscellaneous crowd at the masculine game of cricket, and be with difficulty kept from wearing men's apparel by the bare fear of being hooted by that crowd's offended decency. Let our women keep their own places in our homes in this day of growing disregard of the chimeric "moral" influence, and fear lest the men who should take to prayer meetings in the millinery shops, or to forcible expulsion from these and other haunts of our feminine would-be-tyrants, who see our failings so very clearly, but are blinded to their own.

Hot on the coat-tails of this rebuke was an even more scathing article in *The Maryborough and Dunolly Advertiser* on 13 April.[12]

UNTITLED
The Maryborough and Dunolly Advertiser, 13 April 1874

TWO-AND-TWENTY females in white calico skirts, blue and red Garibaldi jackets, and sailor hats, played a cricket match in the Camp Reserve, Sandhurst, on Easter Monday in the presence of a considerable concourse of spectators, who paid an entrance fee to witness this unbecoming spectacle. Fifty years ago, such an exhibition could not have taken place without subjecting all the actresses in it to general scorn and reprobation. But women are falling so rapidly into contempt, and are becoming so unsexed, that such an event as the one referred to excited no more reprehension than does the appearance on the stage of females in a condition nearly bordering on nudity as they can go to without exciting absolute loathing and disgust. This unfeminine trial of masculine skill at Sandhurst, in which frisky matrons took part with forward spinsters, was engaged as—we are told in the cause of "heaven-born charity." Nothing else could extort money from the pockets of the male public, but this unwomanly exhibition on a public holiday.

The end—that of alleviating mental and physical diseases, brought on by disobedience to the law of GOD—is assumed to justify the means. So that you have only to bestow upon any discreditable, unnatural and repulsive act, the epithet of "charitable," and is held to be perfectly allowable. By-and-bye, perhaps, we shall see the most abominable vices perpetrated in the name of "charity," or almsgiving—for this is the modern and perverted interpretation of the original word; and we shall hear it said of some notorious courtesan, "She leads an infamous life, it is true. Her wealth, which is enormous, is entirely derived from the pollution of her person. But then she builds churches, supports missions, founds alms-houses, endows hospitals, and contributes liberally to Bible and tract societies, and such like 'good works', so as she deserves to be enrolled among the saints on earth, and having 'a saving faith'—she is sure to be admitted to Heaven when she dies."

The *Bendigo Advertiser* tells us that when the cricket match was finished, the players were publicly "thanked for the successful effort which they had made on behalf of the charities, and the gentlemen present sang 'They are jolly good fellows.'" Quite so, the game could not have had a more appropriate finale.

John Rae immediately came to the defence of the women and wrote to both newspapers. He soon became a target, the responses attacking his character along with the reputations of the women cricketers. *The Herald* named their next article on 16 April 'Rae'.[13] *The Maryborough and Dunolly Advertiser* carried on *The Herald's* crusade and a few days later launched a tirade on the ills of John Rae, the cricketers, the people who watched the match and, above all, how they were displeasing God by their actions.[14]

RAE.
The Herald, 16 April 1874

Mr. John Rae appears to be a teacher at the "Ironbark National Common School, No. 323. Established 1861. Bon Accord street, Sandhurst." This is a fact we were not aware of until this morning, when a letter, abounding in the most irate expressions, and written in a very nice schoolboy's hand, arrived by post prepaid. Indeed, we were not aware previously that there was such a person as John Rae, and were quite oblivious of the educational advantages supplied by the "Ironbark National Common School, No. 323. Established 1861. Bon Accord street, Sandhurst." That these advantages are great we gather from the extremely elegant Billingsgate which the teacher sends us in faultless calligraphy.

But let us explain. Lately, there appeared an article in *The Herald* headed "Woman." In the course of this, reference of a deprecatory character, was made to the unseemly exhibition which twenty-two ladies—we will not follow the example of Mr. Rae and question their right to the title—recently made of themselves at Sandhurst, when they indulged, before a mixed company of spectators, in a cricketing contest. Mr. Rae's wife and Mr. Rae's daughters seem to have been the moving spirits in this affair, and to do them justice, made runs with a grace that did them credit, but for all that we are sorry for Mr. Rae. Some kind friend sent a copy of *The Herald*, with the article in question specially marked, to Mrs. Rae. Hence the anger of the gentle teacher, who from birching dirty children seems to think it is but one step, and that an easy one, to enable him to birch other people.

Here is Mr. Rae's pleasant manner of expressing himself:—

> "The green-eyed monster of jealousy has aroused some female creature, stunted and crippled alike in body and mind, to make a contemptible exhibition of herself and degrade the columns of even a paltry paper with gossip as false as it is contemptible."

Well done Rae. We are not aware of any female jealousy, and should be very sorry to think that any of our lady friends are jealous of Mr. Rae's wife and daughters. If we mistake not most of them can bear, with commendable resignation, even the thought that the cricketing ladies are entitled to the happiness of the company of the male Rae while life lasts. It is a hard thought, but still after a fierce struggle we fancy a condition of peaceful resignation could be arrived at even under these painful circumstances.

But seriously, Mr. Rae's wife and daughters have a hard duty before them. The estimable head of the family should be looked after closely, or he will get into some mischief. He will not allow a newspaper to hold and express the opinion that playing cricket before a motley crowd is not calculated to render women more fit for the duties appertaining to their sex. He will not allow us to think that such exhibitions, even under the guise of charity, are indelicate, imprudent, and abominable to the well-balanced mind.

"Charity," it is said, "covers a multitude of sins." This may not be a sin, but certainly in this case charity covers one unseemliness, with this wholesome truth, and the advice to keep his Billingsgate for his own sphere, where, no doubt, it would be received with the appreciation it deserves from those who understand the language, we leave Mr. Rae.

UNTITLED
The Maryborough and Dunolly Advertiser,
20 April 1874

We have received from Mr. John Rae, who dates his letter from the National Common School, No. 323, Bon Accord-street, Sandhurst, the following elegant epistle:—

"Sir—Some one has taken the liberty of thrusting a disgusting publication on my wife and daughter, called the *Maryborough and Dunolly Advertiser*, with an article on the ladies' cricket match specially marked. When I require the services of a degraded and contemptible scoundrel to show my family the evil effects of experiential personal acquaintance with notorious courtesans, I will know where to apply, but meantime they are under my care, and are accustomed to associate with those whose principles are altogether beyond the reach and conception of a vulgar and scurrilous newsmonger."

We hope this is not the style in which he sets copy-book lessons to the little boys and girls under his tuition, and that the irascibility of his temper finds vent in his hours of recreation and in his private correspondence only. We can assure Mr. Rae that there is not a single word of the article which has roused his ire that we wish to retract or modify. We repeat that the female cricket match at Sandhurst was a most unwomanly, discreditable, and reprehensible proceeding; and one which exhibited the decadence of the weaker sex most prominently and painfully.

Our strictures were felt to be just and true by those against whom they were directed, and therefore Mr Rae and his friends winced under them. They struck home. We placed our finger on an ugly sore, and the patient quivered beneath the touch. If our animadversions had been either "vulgar" or "scurrilous," they would have merely fallen pointless and harmless on the object of them, but would have recoiled upon ourselves.

Another correspondent, writing from Sandhurst, makes use of language a little less violent than Mr. Rae's and says:—

> "I think, sir, you know little or nothing of those whom you write, or you would not have used language calculated to damage the character of virtuous and highly respectable ladies.
>
> "The Easter fair committee had decided upon not holding a bazaar in connection with the fair this year, and the ladies not wishing to be prevented from aiding the cause of the 'heaven-born charity,' mooted the idea of a cricket match: as, in default of the bazzar, some means must be used 'to extract money from the pockets of the male public' in support of institutions like the hospital and benevolent asylum.
>
> "I can assure you, sir, that our ladies are far from 'falling into contempt or becoming unsexed' in consequence of their appearing in a cricket match, or what you

are pleased to call 'unwomanly exhibition on a public holiday,'—and I believe had you seen 'the two-and-twenty females in white calico skirts and blue and red Garibaldi jackets,' you would have thought so, too, and would have been ashamed to have written or published such an article.

"The ladies whom you stigmatise as frisky matrons and forward spinsters and compare with actresses in a state of 'almost absolute nudity,' and courtesans are of unblemished character and unimpeachable conduct.

"In conclusion, sir, I trust you will insert this, and thus atone for the insult and slur which you have unwittingly offered to the fair fame of the ladies of Sandhurst."

—J.P.W.

Upon this, it is only necessary to remark that whatever damage has been done to "the characters of virtuous and highly respectable ladies," as our correspondent calls them, has been inflicted by themselves. They played the cricket match, and not we. They consented to constitute themselves a public spectacle and a holiday-show; and not we. They engaged in an unfeminine trial of skill and strength, in the midst of a large concourse of applauding spectators; and not we. They came out from the privacy of domestic life, and challenged criticism and censure; and must be prepared, therefore, to take the consequences.

Our correspondent reiterates that assertion that this unwomanly performance was undertaken in the cause of what he calls "Heaven-born charity." Is he capable of imagining for a moment that what human beings call "charity," namely almsgiving and donations and subscriptions to hospitals and other "benevolent" institutions, is "Heaven-born"? The charity spoken of in the New Testament is Love—that love which does not exist upon the earth—that love, which if it were manifested in human beings towards each other, would preclude the possibility of disease, want, or suffering of any kind.

And, as regards the relief of distress, what was the injunction of our Lord?— "When thou doest thine alms do not sound a trumpet before thee,"—do not march on to a cricket field two and two, in calico skirts, blue and red Garibaldi jackets, and sailor hats, "as the hypocrites do in synagogues, and in the corners of the streets, that they may have glory of men," and be made the subject of foolish poems and fulsome flattery in local newspapers. "Verily I say unto you they have their reward. But when thou doest thine alms, *let not thy left hand know what thy right hand doeth*: that thine alms may be in secret; and thy Father which seeth in secret shall reward thee openly."

Will either of our correspondents venture to affirm that the unnatural cricket match at Sandhurst was played in obedience to this Divine Command? Will they dispute that it was anything else but a display of feminine vanity, frivolity and coquetry, inspired by the greed of admiration and of notoriety, and speciously disguised in the cloak of "Heaven-born charity"? Can they conceive of the mother of our Lord, and his mother's sister, and a score of the women of Nazareth, or of Bethlehem, taking part in a performance of this kind, under any pretence or for any purpose? Can they picture the Son of Man and his disciples forming part of the ring of spectators which gathered round this repulsive spectacle at Sandhurst on Easter Monday, and indulging in the coarse jests and innuendoes which pass from mouth to mouth on such occasions?

A gushing writer for the *Bendigo Evening Star*, represents the wife of our more irate correspondent as returning thanks for the compliments received in the manner following:—

Then Mrs. Rae made answer clear,

"For fame or thanks we came not here;
But now a cause we all revere
Calls out to us for aid.

While fathers on a sick bed lie,
To win the bread poor mothers try;
But children hungry round them cry—
And for their sakes we played.

Not for the game itself we care,
Some bumps and jeers we had to dare;
Yet Charity with pleading prayer,
Urged not her claim in vain.

Your thanks we kindly take;
And when an effort next you make
For Charity the Angel's sake,
We'll do our best again."

And how do the two-and-twenty she-cricketers "revere the cause" referred to in the foregoing jingle? Do they quietly and unostentatiously visit these fathers lying upon a sick bed? Do they carry food to these children, who are crying with hunger? Do they strive to lighten and brighten the daily lives of the destitute and afflicted? Do they endeavour to mitigate the squalor and wretchedness which are to be met within the abodes of the very poor? Do they cheer and encourage such as are struggling with misfortune?

Do they alleviate by kindly talk, by eager service, and by a thousand devices born of active sympathy, the tedium of those who are stretched upon a bed in sickness? Nothing of the sort. "Benevolence," as it is called, must be transacted vicariously, by hireling hands in costly and wasteful institutions. The "Heaven-born charity"—as it is blasphemously called—of the female athletes of Sandhurst expresses itself in the act of two-and-twenty "frisky matrons" and "forward spinsters" engaging in an unwomanly game, in the presence of a multitude of holiday makers, while—[then] as we learn from the versifier in the *Bendigo Evening Star*—"plaudits rent the skies."

Such charity is quite upon par with that of the managers of the Theatre Royal, Melbourne, when they advertise a performance for the benefit of a widow, and pocket the lion's share of the proceeds. "Don't you think," observes Lady Teazle to the Pharisee who has been endeavouring to seduce her, and who brags of his honour, "Don't you think we may as well leave honour out of the argument?" And so we say to the female cricketers of Sandhurst, don't you think that, the next time you exhibit yourselves in public, it would be as well to drop the words "Heaven-born charity" out of the programme?

The *Ballarat Courier* came to the women's defence, claiming they could see nothing unfeminine about women playing cricket. *The Herald* replied:[15]

UNTITLED *(extract)*
The Herald, 25 April 1874

Our premises were that cricket matches, played in public by ladies, could not possibly do any good, and that the exposure of the players to the jests and applause of a motley throng was sure to make them less fitted for the noble duties of the wife, the mother and the sister.

Carry on this cricketing experiment, and the results will be disastrous to women's best interest. From blushing at the jibes and jokes of unknown beholders she will come to regard them in the same platonic light as male cricketers do, and, eventually will not think she exceeds bounds when she answers them. She will then acquire a confidence in her colloquial, as well as physical powers that must be unenviable because unnatural.

We are all content with women as they are, and we are sure the great majority of women are content with the position occupied by their sex.

The newspaper battles between *The Maryborough and Dunolly Advertiser*, *Bendigo Advertiser*, *The Herald* and *The Ballarat Courier* lasted a further full month. Other newspapers around the country, however, stuck to reporting news of the match, often reprinting the original favourable report from the *Bendigo Advertiser*.

OFF THE FIELD

News of the Sandhurst match appeared in city and regional newspapers across Australia. In the Victorian town of Steiglitz (near Geelong), the news was well-received and inspired a women's cricket match played for charity in late May. Some of the community had misgivings but once the match was played, those prejudices dissolved.[16] The *Geelong Advertiser* notes: 'Our correspondent, who is himself a cricketer of no mean repute, seems to have been quite taken aback by the skill displayed by the twenty-two "Graces".'[17] The article doesn't state the correspondent's name, although it could be surmised to have been Tom Wills, as he was a noted cricketer in Geelong at the time and keen to support the women cricketers. In October, another charity match was played in Dural, New South Wales. Once again, the commentary provided by the local newspaper was complimentary, stating, 'It was surprising to see how well the women managed aspects of the game.'[18]

Word about the Sandhurst match reached the fair shores of England, also in the form of reprints of the original complimentary post-match summary from the *Bendigo Advertiser*.[19] News also made it to America, appearing in the *New Orleans Republican*, the *Public Ledger [Memphis, Tennessee]*, and many more newspapers published overseas.[20]

Even though there had been reports of women's cricket being played competitively in the United Kingdom since 1745, the games and reports appear to be spasmodic and irregular. More than a century later, news of the Australian women cricketers appeared to inspire a resurgence. Mrs TB Harrup from New Inn, Nash, put a notice in the *Buckingham Advertiser and Free Press* on 15 August 1874: 'The Nash ladies are open to play 11 ladies of any town or village in the County of Buckinghamshire.'[21] The callout was successful and the match was played before an interested crowd. The Nash ladies scored 115 in one innings while their opponents only scored 86 in two innings.[22]

While the news of a women's cricket match in Sandhurst generated scorn in the Melbourne press, elsewhere it was reported with interest, enthusiasm and as a source of inspiration.

WOMEN'S RIGHTS AND MEN'S WRONGS

In 1875, the *Melbourne Punch* published two full page illustrations titled 'Women's Rights' and 'Men's Wrongs' (Figures 15 and 16) with no other commentary other than the five points of text that accompanied each image. The images show the difficulties faced by women attempting to be recognised, and the resistance by some at the time. This was an attitude often presented by men but also supported by many other women.

WOMEN'S RIGHTS.
Melbourne Punch, 30 December 1875

1. *Emily.*—"Do you know, Mabel, since I have taken up the cares and worries of business, my hair has come out dreadfully."
   Mabel.—"So has mine, dear. It never used to before I took my proper place in Henry's counting-house and placed Henry at home in his.
   Henry (nursing the baby).—"Y-e-s, my dear, I've no-noticed it too; in fact, I've often thought of telling you how much you and Emily look like a couple of Ce-Celestials." (A scene.)
2. THE VERANDAH RING. The "doves and the ducks" take the places of the "bulls and the bears."
3. The Curtain Lecture. *Mr Jones.*—"Stuff and nonsense, your Parliamentary duties *do not* keep you out till four in the morning—it's that horrid Yorick Club—that's what it is, and no one will ever make me believe different. Besides, Mrs. J., you were *not sober* when you came in!"

FIGURE 15 Women's Rights. *Melbourne Punch*, 1875.

4. A Pretty "Cut," in a pretty costume. (Woman's proper "sphere" is undoubtedly the cricket ball.)
5. *Sweet girl graduate.*—"'Spinster of arts' would never do, my dears—'bachelor of arts' we reject with scorn—there is but one thing for it, we must fall back on our proper title in full, *Baccalaurea Artium*, until someone can give us a decent feminine equivalent for bachelor."

MEN'S WRONGS.
Melbourne Punch, 30 December 1875

---

1. THE SEWING CIRCLE. Husbands of the future enjoy tea and scandal while their wives are "under the verandah."
2. The happy pair!! "Remember, sir, you have promised to love, honour, and obey, and I'll see you do." (Nurse on the left tries to make a little hay while the (honey-moon shines).
3. Wife: "Chops again to-day—I can get a better dinner at the Club."
   Husband *(meekly):* I'm very sorry, dear, but it's washing day: I couldn't mind the baby and cook any better dinner." (Bursts into tears).
4. Mrs Jones: "Pray *how much* longer are you going to keep me waiting?"

FIGURE 16 Men's Wrongs. *Melbourne Punch*, 1875.

> Mr J.: "I'm hurrying as quick as I can. I'll be ready in a minute, my love. I couldn't get my whiskers to set right."

5. When all these things take place, i.e., when woman gets *her* rights, it will be much better for poor injured man to purchase a tail, discard his wearing apparel, grow his natural covering, take his pipe and tobacco (the only real gift of civilisation) go back into the wilderness and be an ancestor again. We mean to.

A SECOND INNINGS FOR SANDHURST

Surprisingly, the Sandhurst ladies agreed to play another match at the 1875 Sandhurst Easter Fair. The advertisements appeared in mid-March, with Barbara Rae once again calling for women cricketers.

On 30 March, the day of the parade, it must have felt like deja vu for the cricketers. The weather was once again overcast with rain in the morning, and the teams wore the same style uniforms as the previous year – full-length calico dress with a jacket of either pink or blue. However, as the parade was due to start, the rain stopped and the clouds cleared. Like the preceding year, the day became warm after a crisp morning.

This time, the cricketers were the stand-out participants in the parade. The ornate carriages they rode in were drawn by magnificent horses and accompanied by two outriders. Representing the respective eleven riding in their carriage, one carriage driver wore a jacket of yellow and blue and a green cap with a gold band, and the other wore a cerise jacket and similar cap.[23]

At one o'clock the following day, the day of the match, the carriages returned to Ironbark School to collect the cricketers. They did a short tour of the city, with plenty of spectators turning out to watch them pass by. When they arrived at the ground, the respective captains led the march onto the field, arms linked once again, one pink one blue, to the beat of a drum. The Reds were captained by Miss Murdoch and the team also included Miss Midwinter, sister to the famous male cricketer Billy Midwinter, and the Blues were once again led by Barbara Rae. The ladies assembled and the Reds went in to bat.

The *Bendigo Advertiser* on 1 April describes the women as playing with great skill.[24] The article also defends the women's dignity, referring to the criticisms from the previous year's assaults by the press. The article recounts a number of highlights of the match, including Miss Midwinter's score of 24 runs. The highest score, however, went to Miss Glen, who carried out her bat at the end of the second innings after scoring 34 runs to great cheering from the crowd. Miss Gerber was also celebrated for her bowling prowess as she took seven wickets, plus caught one out in the second innings.

Gerber's bowling was compared to the veteran cricketer Wills, and her pace to that of another cricketer's,

Allan. This was the first time a woman cricket player's skill had been compared to that of a man's, let alone *two* extremely accomplished male cricketers of the time. It was a fitting testament to Gerber's skills indeed.

THE LADIES' CRICKET MATCH.
Bendigo Advertiser, 1 April 1875

For the second time the ladies of Bendigo have dared public opinion, and, putting aside the dogmas of usage, have ventured by that portion generally held to be sacred to the department of the human race which wears trousers. And for the second time they have shown that it is possible for a lady to be a cricketer and still to retain her name. It is well enough for your bilious or sensation-seeking scribe to decry a thing he never saw, but given fair play and honest criticism, and the ladies who have enriched the charities of Bendigo so materially have no fear to dread results.

Indeed the exhibition they made in the field yesterday would go to lead to the belief that the game of cricket is completely compassable by the female form, and very possibly by the female intellect. As a matter of fact those who saw two or three of the ladies, and notably Miss Gerber bowl yesterday must have been satisfied that in the ranks of the present practisers of the game there are those who might shine with bat, ball, or gloves even when put in competition with some of the elevens turned out by the presumedly superior sex. The young ladies have evidently been trained in all sorts of play; they are fair fielders, some of them bowl well, and more than half a dozen know the virtue of a straight bat.

The play yesterday was commenced very shortly after the announced time; the Hon. Angus Mackay standing umpire at one end, and at the commencement Mr. J. Hechle at the other. This was through the non-arrival of the Hon. J. J. Casey, Minister of Lands. Mr. Latham, however, at an early period of the game relieved Mr. Hechle from his most onerous duties. It would only tire our readers were they to be taken through the game technically from its start to its finish. Indeed, a labored description of a match of the sort is hardly possible.

Let it be said that there were two special features in the day's play. The one, the batting of Miss Midwinter; the other, the bowling of Miss Gerber. The former young lady has comparatively all her brother's mastery of the ball at the wickets. Her defence is good, and she is besides a very powerful hitter. She made one clean drive for 1 yesterday under the chains, which even Beswick might have envied. Nor was the bowling opposed to her at all to be despised, for Miss Gerber has pitch, pace—when she wants it—and patience. Almost always on the spot she varies her bowling with the astuteness of a veteran like Wills, and her pace with the rarity of a demon like Allan. Indeed Miss Gerber, with a good field behind her, would be a dangerous opponent anywhere. Her fielding, too, was excessively good. There were numerous other points in the play which would call for comment were it not that in these cases to particularise is to be invidious. With regard to the match, indeed Shakespeare might be quoted, and one may be allowed—paraphrasing him slightly—to say, "For its own person it beggared all description."

No one could have watched the healthful glow on the cheeks of the young ladies who were engaged in the match yesterday without feeling assured that cricket carried out purely and simply is a game as conducive to health as anything; and moreover a game as easily played by ladies as croquet. During the whole day's play, there was no show of ungracefulness. Of course, at times, the field got disorganised, and long leg found herself in a place more like mid-off; but still the mistakes made were few, and by no means frequent.

At point, the two ladies who filled the position for their respective teams were especially good; while, in the bowling department, it is doubtful whether a second eleven of the B.U.C.C. could excel the precision and judgment of Miss Gerber and the other ladies who trundled at the wickets—and with good success, too. Catches were "like angels visits, few and far between;" but then, the chances given were neither numerous nor easy. So it may be said that the Ladies' Cricket Match of 1875 was a grand success; and we may all join in an earnest wish that they will live to play a score more in the cause for which they yesterday exhibited themselves. We subjoin the score:—

REDS.
First Innings.
Miss Petrie, b Westhead	1
Miss Martin, b Shalders	2
Miss Glen, b Westhead	8
Miss Hinton, b Steane	0
Miss Murdoch, b Steane	0
Miss Midwinter, b Gerber	24
Miss Rae, b Shalders	13
Miss R. Shalders, c and b Rae	11
Miss Allpress, run out	0
Miss Lawrence, b Gerber	12
Mrs Hoffner, not out	15
Wide	1
Total	**87**

BLUES.
First Innings.
Miss Hughes, b N. Rae 4
Miss Leyshon, c Petrie, b Murdoch 5
Mrs. Koenig, b Murdoch 0
Miss Hinton, b Petrie 1
Miss Gerber, b Petrie 5
Miss B. Rae, b N. Rae 7
Miss C. Snowden, b Murdoch 11
Miss Steane, not out 13
Miss Lewis, b N. Rae 1
Miss Westhead, b Petrie 9
Miss S. Allpress, b Petrie 7
Wides 2
Total 65

REDS.
Second Innings.
Miss Petrie, b Gerber 10
Miss Midwinter, b Gerber 17
Miss Martin, b Gerber 0
Miss N. Rae, b Gerber 0
Miss R. Shalders, b Steane, c Gerber 0
Miss Allpress, b Gerber 0
Miss Lawrence, run out 5
Miss Glen, not out 34
Mrs. Hoffner, c and b Westhead 6
Miss Hinton, b Gerber 1
Miss Murdoch, b Gerber 3
Wide 1
Total 77

The match, having started somewhere between one and two o'clock, finished around six o'clock as day turned to dusk. The Reds scored 87 over two innings and the Blues 65 over one, with the onset of evening offering no chance for the Blues to attempt a victory. Some reports cited crowds were in excess of 2,000 people, while *The Age* states there were 5,000 people watching the women's cricket.[25] Either way, the turnout was exceptional.

In another account of the 1875 match, a BUCC member [name not given] revealed how the ladies came to play in 1874. John Rae, wife of Emily and father to Nellie and Barbara Rae, had the idea to host a 'muff' match between the ministers of the various churches and the male teachers in the area, but the clergy issued a rebuff for Rae's unintentional offence to the dignity of the cloth. Having already resolved to assist the charities by organising a cricket match, Rae turned to the ladies to assist.[26]

Whatever the driving force that assembled the team, this second match was a significant success for Sandhurst and the women cricketers – maybe even more than the first. It demonstrated that the women knew how to play and were skilled and serious players.

> ***THE LADIES' CRICKET MATCH.***
> ***(BY A MEMBER OF THE B.U.C.C.)***
> ***(extract)*** *Bendigo Advertiser*, 3 April 1875
>
> ---
>
> Who want's to know where worth is found,
> For what he wants to pay,

> Go to the Back Cricket Ground,
> And see the ladies play.
> The sight the saddest heart will cheer,
> And chase away your care;
> The ladies match must be this year,
> The flower o' all the Fair.
> The ladies seek not for applause,
> For honor, or for fame,
> But only aid a noble cause
> By playing a noble game.

POST-MATCH WIND-UP

The news once again lit up the colonies. On 1 April, *The Age* was quick off the mark with a highly complimentary article summarising the match, calling it the 'greatest success in connection with the Easter festivities'.[27] Also appearing in the commercial section of *The Age* was the news from its Sandhurst correspondent that: 'Not a single sale was recorded, and after twelve o'clock the place was deserted, everybody going off to see the ladies' cricket match.'[28] The same day, *The Herald* article appeared, full of wrath, as if they'd been waiting for an entire year to have another go.[29]

LADY CRICKETERS.
The Herald, 1 April 1875

In noticing the unseemly exhibition at Back Creek yesterday when "For Charity's Sake," twenty-two females "exhibited as cricketers," our contemporary the Advertiser appears sorely astonished at the conduct of certain young gentleman who had gone there just as they would to the stalls of a theatre when a leg piece is on.

A great deal of fuss has been made of late years, "cries the Advertiser," concerning the increase of what is termed larrikinism, but we believe that a grosser exhibition than that witnessed on the Back Creek Cricket ground yesterday has not been perpetrated in Sandhurst for many a day, and that by individuals from whom better manners might be expected. A gang of young men were to be seen knocking about the reserve all day, and the manner in which they conducted themselves was simply disgraceful. All sorts of remarks were made concerning the performance of the young ladies who agreed to play cricket in public for a noble cause, and considering that the observations made were to be heard nearly all over the ground the wonder is that the players did not immediately retire from the circle. Under no circumstances, but more particularly under those of yesterday, could the conduct of the persons indicated be excused, and no amount of explanation could remove the stigma cast upon them by every right-thinking man on the ground.

We won't attempt to defend the youngsters, but we must say the "lady" cricketers had no reason to complain. They paraded their ankles to the public gaze, and if Crisp, the banker's clerk, observed to Jones, the draper that Miss So-and so's feet were of the beetle-crusher order, or that Mrs Such a one's understandings were those of a Mullingar butler, "beef to the heels," they only indulged in criticism on the exhibit specially provided for them, just as they would when viewing a "leg piece" unmercifully castigate the ill-made members of the corps de ballet.

The draw at this cricket match, call it "for charity's sake" as you will, was identically the same as that at a burlesque or such as we were acquainted with in this city some years ago when Oriental cafes and the like were the rage. And yet our poor contemporary is astonished, and rises up to curse the young rascals who paid their money to see the sight, and undoubtedly had a right to criticise.

Rather the *Advertiser* should have struck at the root of the evil and repudiated such exhibitions, which are lowering to the females engaged and depraving to the young spectators of the other sex.

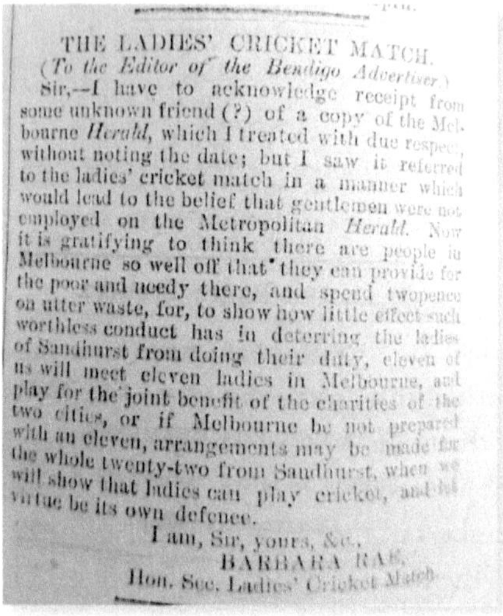

THE LADIES' CRICKET MATCH.
(To the Editor of the Bendigo Advertiser.)

Sir,—I have to acknowledge receipt from some unknown friend (?) of a copy of the Melbourne *Herald*, which I treated with due respect, without noting the date; but I saw it referred to the ladies' cricket match in a manner which would lead to the belief that gentlemen were not employed on the Metropolitan *Herald*. Now it is gratifying to think there are people in Melbourne so well off that they can provide for the poor and needy there, and spend twopence on utter waste, for, to show how little effect such worthless conduct has in deterring the ladies of Sandhurst from doing their duty, eleven of us will meet eleven ladies in Melbourne, and play for the joint benefit of the charities of the two cities, or if Melbourne be not prepared with an eleven, arrangements may be made for the whole twenty-two from Sandhurst, when we will show that ladies can play cricket, and let virtue be its own defence.

I am, Sir, yours, &c.,
BARBARA RAE,
Hon. Sec. Ladies' Cricket Match.

FIGURE 17 Letter from Barbara Rae. *Bendigo Advertiser*, 6 April 1875.

> "For virtue's sake" let us hope we have heard the last of Ladies' Cricket Matches, unless the intention is that ballet girls should forsake the clerically condemned stage, and show their legs on the cricket field, with Ministers of Mines and Lands to sanctify the scene by their presence, and a Bendigo Advertiser to wail over the depravity of the genteel youth of the opposite sex, because they will rather criticise the ladies rather than watch their play.

The Herald insisted the ladies shouldn't be showpieces and that if anyone in the crowd behaved poorly – as was suggested in some reports – then the women should be held to account for others' bad behaviour.[30] This provoked Barbara Rae to speak up, sending a letter to the editor at the *Bendigo Advertiser* in which she invited eleven Melbourne ladies to form a team and join their efforts to play for charity (Figure 17).

The Argus replied to Barbara Rae's letter immediately, publishing its reply the next day:[31]

> **UNTITLED (extract)**
> *The Argus*, 7 April 1875
>
> We hope the ladies of Melbourne will not respond to that invitation, and we venture to suggest that the ladies of Sandhurst should confine their cricket playing to their own locality.

The Melbourne *Leader*, however, was all for a Melbourne match:[32]

CRICKET GOSSIP.
Leader, 10 April 1875

It [cricket] is a game of skill, and not one in which mere brute strength carries the sway, and in point of skill ladies have before now shown themselves well in the front. Those who object to the game as unsuitable cannot cavil when twenty-two ladies have the courage to face a crowd in aid of the helpless and destitute. The match will be a great novelty, and if attended by fine weather will draw thousands of people.

These articles highlight the conflict that was arising over the role of women in society, but predominantly from a male perspective. It appeared that even though city dwellers were regarded as being more sophisticated and advanced, in the case of women and cricket, it was the people of regional areas who demonstrated a more progressive attitude.

About the same time Barbara Rae's letter challenging Melbourne to a match was published, a separate letter was sent by the secretary of the Easter Fair – presumably Robert Denyer – suggesting a charity match be organised in Melbourne between the Sandhurst and Melbourne ladies as a fundraiser for their respective local hospitals. The Melbourne Hospital committee did not respond to the letter directly, choosing instead to publish a reply in *The Age*, where it stated the communication had been received, with 'the committee not deeming it advisable to take action in the matter'.[33]

Barbara Rae's offer was received much more keenly by Tom Wills in Geelong. Wills was famous in the colonies for his own cricketing prowess. On hearing of the committee's rebuff to the Sandhurst ladies, Wills wrote to Barbara Rae, asking her to bring her twenty-two to Geelong.[34] Unfortunately, not long after Wills's intentions were printed, another note was published saying Wills was having some trouble finding a team of Geelong ladies willing to play the Sandhurst lady cricketers.[35]

On 26 April, a letter from Barbara Rae was published attesting that due to the uncertainty of the weather, the cricketers would not be visiting Geelong this season, 'But if they make an early start next season, Geelong will not be forgotten.'[36]

Nothing more was heard of women's competitive cricket in Sandhurst until 30 December 1875, when a ladies' match was scheduled on the Kangaroo Flat ground on New Year's Day at one o'clock. There was no follow-up report of the match so it's not known if it actually went ahead, or if it did, which of the ladies may have played.

FIGURE 18 Fernleas and Siroccos.
Australian Town and Country Journal, 17 April 1886.

ALL OUT

There's no account of the Rae women, or any of the Sandhurst women, playing a match again. In February 1878, a comment from the hospital committee asking if the secretary would write to John Rae and request the ladies appear for a cricket match at the upcoming Easter Fair, appeared in the *Bendigo Advertiser*. It can only be assumed that the answer was no.

Yet, even though the women didn't play again, they had set a new standard: they had shown that women *could* play cricket and that they could play it *well*. And, if they had only known how far news of their endeavours would travel over the coming years, and how it was an inspiration to many other women, maybe they would have kept on playing.

In 1885, ten years after the second Sandhurst match, a women's cricket club was re-established in England. In Australia in 1886, two women's teams – the Fernleas and Siroccos – played at the Sydney Cricket Ground to a crowd of 1,000 spectators (Figure 18).[37] In New South Wales, women's cricket appeared to be gaining acceptance. Matches continued to be played competitively.

In Victoria, however, it seemed things had gone backwards. Novelty matches played in society circles graced the pages of the newspapers: men playing against women with the men playing left-handed or with broomsticks or with pick handles (Figure 19).[38]

In 1888, Queen Victoria dedicated half a column each week in a London newspaper to ladies' cricket.[39]

FIGURE 19 Women cricketers.
The Australasian, 1 December 1888.

Two years later – things did move slowly – *The Age* reported that London was considering sending their women cricketers to Australia.[40] For whatever the reason, the English team never made it to Australia at this time (Figure 20). However, the intent and enthusiasm generated was sufficient to encourage Australian women to pick up a bat and play. In October 1890, advertisements appeared in *The Herald* calling for the formation of a ladies' cricket club.[41] By November of that year, teams from two newly formed women's clubs, Fitzroy and South Melbourne, had played a competitive game of cricket at Albert Park.[42] Sixteen years after that first Australian match in Sandhurst, it appeared that Melbournians had changed their view.

In December 1890, women's cricket once again hit the Australian news. In a match at the Sydney Cricket Ground in New South Wales between the Probables and the Sydney Club, the Probables scored a total of 321, of which Rosalie Deane of New South Wales scored a whopping 195.[43]

In 1891, the first women's intercolonial match was played between New South Wales and Victoria at the Sydney Cricket Ground. There were low crowd numbers and all sorts of problems with teams being short of players and players disputing payments and, considering the significance of the event, it was barely mentioned in the newspapers.[44] The match was called a failure. However, it didn't stop the women from continuing to play. In 1893 (Figure 21), it appeared cricket was again socially acceptable in Adelaide.

FIGURE 20 The women cricketers at Liverpool, England. *The Sydney Mail and New South Wales Advertiser*, 21 June 1890.

In Melbourne in March 1895, two teams of eleven – one from New South Wales and one from Victoria – played in a match at the East Melbourne Cricket Ground. The match was organised by Ellie Finkelstein, honourable secretary of the Fitzroy Ladies' Cricket Club.[45] Interestingly, the team names were the Reds and the Blues.

This match received a full-page pictorial spread in the *Weekly Times* (Figure 22).

THE MAIDENS OVER

It seems many connections to early women's cricket history, the Sandhurst games and probably plenty more have been lost – even in family histories. Perhaps, sadly, the women players decided it was a shame rather than a success to have participated in the matches at all. This is why sharing their stories is so important.

There is a rather interesting connection from the past to the present, one that honours a family line. Bear with me as we trace the Rae family tree.

John Rae married Helen Fincher in 1852. Barbara Rae was born in 1855, and Nellie in 1860. Helen died in 1864 and John remarried Emily Stuart Stocks. Mrs Emily Rae, the 1874 captain of the Reds, died in 1881 in Lorne.[46] In that same year, Barbara Rae, captain of the Blues in 1874 and 1875, married John Archibald and moved to Bairnsdale. She died ten years after Emily in 1891, aged 36.[47]

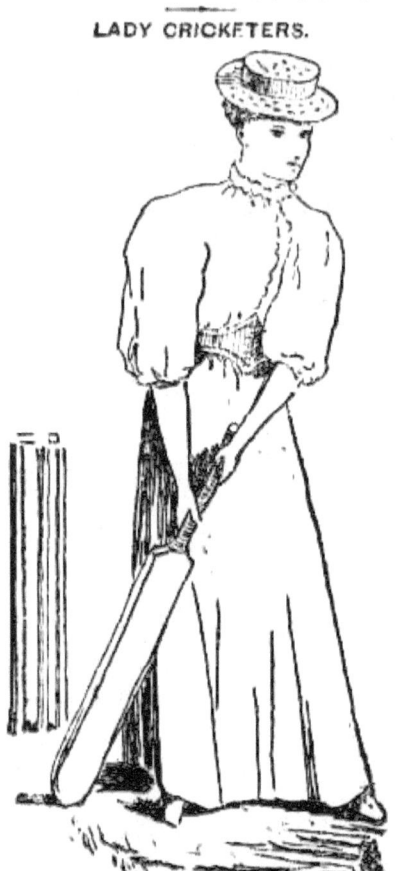

FIGURE 21 The batswoman.
Adelaide Observer, 16 December 1893.

John Rae moved to Melbourne and became a headmaster of Port Melbourne State School. He died in 1894.[48]

Helen (Nellie), a player in both the 1874 and 1875 games, married in 1883, when Barbara was still alive, and Barbara was one of her bridesmaids.[49] Helen's husband was Edward James (EJ) Cordner. EJ Cordner died in 1930, and Helen 22 years later in 1952 at 92 years of age.[50]

The family tree and Cordner name goes on to follow a strong sporting family line of Australian Rules footballers. Helen and Edward's son, Edward Rae, was the father of Don Cordner, the 1946 VFL Brownlow medallist.[51]

With a surprising current-day twist, Harriet Cordner, already a fourth-generation Melbourne Football Club representative, is also a direct descendant of a founding player in the first women's cricket match in Australia: the great-great-granddaughter of Helen 'Nellie' Rae.

To conclude this book about the first games of women's competitive cricket in Australia, here's a delightfully eloquent article by 'Queen Bee', journalist Jessie Grover, on the topic.[52]

And, did you know over-arm bowling was invented by a woman? Who would have thought…?

CRICKET FOR LADIES.
BY QUEEN BEE.
The Australasian, 29 January 1887

When lawn tennis was first introduced, at once there arose a number of severe critics,

FIGURE 22 Women's cricket in 1895, at the East Melbourne Cricket Ground. *Weekly Times,* 23 March 1895.

who, from a standpoint of sublime ignorance, denounced the game as "childish, and about on a par with battledore and shuttlecock." They said that the game was "too ridiculous, and its devotees were donkeys." For a time, it seemed as if these clever persons were to be on the right side for once, as lawn tennis or "Badminton," as it was originally called, kept under a cloud, and gave little promise of the great favourite it would become in the near future. But the reaction came, and now there are few who will dispute the fact that lawn tennis is the best open-air pastime ever invented for both sexes to play. Without an effort it has thoroughly eclipsed croquet and archery, and the prophets have retired discomfited.

It is always so easy to find fault, to be a critic,

> "A man must serve his time to every trade.
> Save censure – critics are already made,"

sings Lord Byron; and here and there one still finds people who cannot even now, for the life of them, see "anything in tennis or cricket – or, indeed, in any outdoor game." These delightful creatures are always non-players. Outdoor games were never invented for old people, or independent persons, or for that species of humanity known as "stout parties." Not only is tennis a thoroughly healthy game, but it is the best exercise for the limbs and muscles that could possibly be imagined, and, above all, it is a graceful game. Watch a girl who can play either "taking" or "serving," and note the free use of all parts of the body it necessitates, and the graceful positions and poses she assumes. These are the lines we have seen repeatedly in the old Greek sculpture and in the old masters, and we admire them.

All that can be advanced in favour of lawn tennis applies with equal force to cricket. It is a healthy, invigorating, outdoor exercise, and at home seems to be fast making headway. The reason for this, no doubt, is that there are so many houses in England with cricket grounds attached, where the game can be indulged in as privately as tennis is in one's own court.

It is altogether a mistaken idea that women have only taken to cricket of late years. It was a woman who invented round-arm bowling, and Mr. Box in his work on cricket tells us that as far back as 1707 a match was played at Bury between eleven single and eleven married women of the parish, the matrons winning by 80 runs. Matches for money were then common, and in 1811 a game was played between female elevens from Surrey and Hampshire at Ball's Pond for a stake of five hundred guineas. The performers, we are told, were of all ages and sizes; the young wore shawls, and the old players long cloaks. They wore distinguishing colours in their bonnets, but no mention is made of any variation from the ordinary costume of the day.

Ann Baker, a woman of sixty, proved to be the best bowler and runner on the Surrey side, but despite her prowess Hampshire scored the victory. A match between the married and single ladies of Hockwold cum Wilton, in Norfolk, was played in 1823, for eleven pairs of gloves (no mention is made of the number of buttons – a serious omission) and is remarkable for the fact that on this occasion the players wore jackets and trousers, tastefully decorated with blue ribbon. This, then, is the first instance on record of a departure from the ordinary dress worn by women.

The great interest taken of late years by women in the national game of Englishmen has brought about their appearance on the cricket field. They have learned from their male friends all the points of the game, and very naturally they have longed to take a hand in what seems to be one of the good things of this life. So they have ventured forth and enjoyed cricket in their own quiet way. Already there are numbers of girls in this colony who can play well. They have learned it from their brothers gradually. As children they have been called on to "Come and give us a ball or two," and they have ended up by enjoying the evening's practice as well as the boys. Once having learned it, it is difficult to relinquish so fascinating a game when the years of discretion are reached, and why should they? What is there unwomanly in cricket, played in the right place and at proper seasons? "Oh, but," says Mr. Grundy, "there is the dreadful bloomer costume and the playing in public." Tennis is not played in public, neither should cricket be. Any game can be vulgarised by going to extremes." If tennis was played in public in bloomer costume as a draw what would be said of it? Would it be quite fair to blame the game and talk of unwomanliness? Tennis is the steppingstone to cricket and those who can play well at the former game would very soon become proficient at the latter. Of course, there is the bowling to learn, and it is a fact testified to by those who know that women make really excellent bowlers in a very short space of time, as round-arm bowling comes quite naturally to them, for in nine cases out of ten if a woman is asked to throw she will bowl instead.

A sister of the renowned W.G. Grace is said to be one of the best slow bowlers in England, and she can at times send a ball down with such a twist on it that it requires all her brother's skill to keep it from taking his wicket. But the question about all others is, what is the best and most suitable dress for cricket. Is it to be the bloomer costume? The answer is no. The same costume you play lawn tennis in is equally adapted for cricket. Perhaps the skirt might be a trifle shorter, and as, absolute freedom for the arms is necessary, a jersey may be worn. A pair of cricketing shoes—i.e., shoes with spikes in them—is an absolute necessity to prevent slipping.

In commencing there will, no doubt, be some difficulty in keeping skirts out of the wicket, but I do not think it will be an surmountable obstacle, any more than it is for men to keep the thick heavy pads they wear from "playing" the ball. The umpire will have to decide if the skirt stopped the ball, and as there is some probability of the rule in this direction being considerably revised umpires will be allowed full latitude. If the rule is altered as proposed "skirt before wicket" will dismiss many a good batswoman.

FIGURE 23 *Cricket Match Played by the Countess of Derby and Other Ladies 1779, English School.*

FIGURES

1. 1936 'OLD VICTORIAN SCHOOLDAYS', *The Age* (Melbourne, Vic.: 1854–1954), 9 May, p. 8, viewed 20 Feb 2021, http://nla.gov.au/nla.news-article204831568
2. 1864 'CHRISTMAS IN AUSTRALIA', *The Australian News for Home Readers* (Vic.: 1864–1867), 24 December, p. 9, viewed 20 Feb 2021, http://nla.gov.au/nla.news-article63170783
3. Lacy, George. 1860, *The first gathering of the Bendigo Caledonian Society, Jan. 2nd, 1860*, viewed 24 February 2021, http://nla.gov.au/nla.obj-134735938
4. 1874 'Advertising', *Bendigo Advertiser* (Vic.: 1855–1918), 5 March, p. 1, viewed 5 Nov 2019, http://nla.gov.au/nla.news-article88228767
5. 1874 'Advertising', *Bendigo Advertiser* (Vic.: 1855–1918), 13 March, p. 3, viewed 5 Nov 2019, http://nla.gov.au/nla.news-article88229003
6. 1874 'Advertising', *Bendigo Advertiser* (Vic.: 1855–1918), 17 March, p. 3, viewed 20 Feb 2021, http://nla.gov.au/nla.news-article88229120
7. 1895 'MRS. AMELIA BLOOMER', *The Pictorial Australian* (Adelaide, SA: 1885–1895), 1 March, p. 42, viewed 19 Feb 2021, http://nla.gov.au/nla.news-article227747521
8. 1874, 'THE BENDIGO ADVERTISER', *Bendigo Advertiser* (Vic.: 1855–1918), 26 March, p. 2, viewed 7 Nov 2019, http://nla.gov.au/nla.news-article88229342
9. 1874 'No Title', *The Ballarat Courier* (Vic.: 1869–1883; 1914–1918), 28 March, p. 2, viewed 7 Nov 2019, http://nla.gov.au/nla.news-article192285585
10. 1874 'Perfect Loves', *Melbourne Punch* (Vic.: 1855–1900), 26 March, p. 3, viewed 7 Nov 2019, http://nla.gov.au/nla.news-article174547403
11. 1862 Hathi Trust Digital Library, hathitrust.org, 'NEW STYLE ZOUAVE JACKETS', *Godey's Magazine*. v.64 1862 Jan–Jun, viewed 20 Feb 2021, https://babel.hathitrust.org/cgi/pt?id=mdp.39015016441498&view=1up&seq=126

12. 1862 Hathi Trust Digital Library, hathitrust.org, 'THE GARIBALDI SHIRT', *Godey's Magazine*. v.64 1862 Jan–Jun, viewed 20 Feb 2021, https://babel.hathitrust.org/cgi/pt?id=mdp.39015016441498&view=2up&seq=228
13. 1874 'TO-DAY'S EVENTS', *Bendigo Advertiser* (Vic.: 1855–1918), 7 April, p. 2, viewed 7 Nov 2019, http://nla.gov.au/nla.news-article88229600
14. 1874 'CONTENTS OF TO-DAY'S PAPER', *The Argus* (Melbourne, Vic.: 1848–1957), 9 April, p. 6, viewed 7 Nov 2019, http://nla.gov.au/nla.news-article5867565
15. 1875 'WOMEN'S RIGHTS', *Melbourne Punch* (Vic.: 1855–1900), 30 December, p. 11, (PUNCH ALMANAC FOR 1876), viewed 19 Feb 2021, http://nla.gov.au/nla.news-article174632867
16. 1875 'MEN'S WRONGS', *Melbourne Punch* (Vic.: 1855–1900), 30 December, p. 12. (PUNCH ALMANAC FOR 1876), viewed 19 Feb 2021, http://nla.gov.au/nla.news-article174632868
17. 1875 'THE LADIES' CRICKET MATCH', *Bendigo Advertiser* (Vic.: 1855–1918), 6 April, p. 2, viewed 5 Nov 2019, http://nla.gov.au/nla.news-article88257985 (Faint online copy – original newspaper viewed in Victorian State Library Reading Room).
18. 1886 'Sweet Girl Cricketers', *Australian Town and Country Journal* (Sydney, NSW: 1870–1919), 17 April, p. 34, viewed 25 Feb 2021, http://nla.gov.au/nla.news-article71076076
19. 1888 *The Australasian* (Melbourne, Vic.: 1864–1946), 1 December, p. 12, viewed 5 Nov 2019, http://nla.gov.au/nla.news-page15068245
20. 1890 'THE ORIGINAL ENGLISH LADY CRICKETERS AT LIVERPOOL', *The Sydney Mail and New South Wales Advertiser* (NSW: 1871–1912), 21 June, p. 1370, viewed 19 Feb 2021, http://nla.gov.au/nla.news-article162074415
21. 1893 'LADY CRICKETERS', *Adelaide Observer (SA: 1843–1904)*, 16 December, p. 40, viewed 19 Feb 2021, http://nla.gov.au/nla.news-article160818067
22. 1895 'The Ladies' Cricket Match', *Weekly Times* (Melbourne, Vic.: 1869–1954), 23 March, p. 11, viewed 7 Nov 2019, http://nla.gov.au/nla.news-article220539865

23. *Cricket Match Played by the Countess of Derby and Other Ladies 1779,* English School, Viewed 19 Feb 2021, https://upload.wikimedia.org/wikipedia/commons/1/17/Cricket_Match_Played_by_the_Countess_of_Derby_and_Other_Ladies%2C_1779.jpg

ENDNOTES

1. 1874 'THE BENDIGO ADVERTISER', *Bendigo Advertiser* (Vic.: 1855–1918), 19 March, p. 2, viewed 2 July 2019, http://nla.gov.au/nla.news-article88229165

2. 1874 'The Cornwall Chronicle WITH WHICH IS INCORPORATED THE LAUNCESTON TIMES. MONDAY, MARCH 30, 1874', *The Cornwall Chronicle* (Launceston, Tas.: 1835–1880), 30 March, p. 2, viewed 7 Nov 2019, http://nla.gov.au/nla.news-article66077645; 1874 'THE HURRICANE AT WESTWOOD', *Gympie Times and Mary River Mining Gazette* (Qld.: 1868–1919), 4 April, p. 4, viewed 7 Nov 2019, http://nla.gov.au/nla.news-article168908646

3. 1874 'EASTER MONDAY', *The Argus* (Melbourne, Vic.: 1848–1957), 7 April, p. 5, viewed 7 Nov 2019, http://nla.gov.au/nla.news-article5867375

4. 1873 'COSTUME CRICKET MATCH', *Leader* (Melbourne, Vic.:1862–1918, 1935), 4 January, p. 10, viewed 2 July 2019, http://nla.gov.au/nla.news-article197926816

5. 1874 'BLUE JACKETS ON SHORE', *Bendigo Advertiser* (Vic.: 1855–1918), 7 April, p. 2, viewed 7 Nov 2019, http://nla.gov.au/nla.news-article88229604

6. 1874 'THE LADIES' CRICKET MATCH', *Bendigo Advertiser* (Vic.: 1855–1918), 8 April, p. 2, viewed 7 Nov 2019, http://nla.gov.au/nla.news-article88229632

7. 1874 'THE EASTER FAIR. SECOND DAY', *Bendigo Advertiser* (Vic.: 1855–1918), 8 April, p. 2, viewed 7 Nov 2019, http://nla.gov.au/nla.news-article88229637

8. 1874 'COMMERCIAL INTELLIGENCE', *The Argus* (Melbourne, Vic.: 1848–1957), 8 April, p. 6, viewed 9 July 2019, http://nla.gov.au/nla.news-article5867467

9. 1874 'THE SECOND BATCH', *Bendigo Advertiser* (Vic.: 1855–1918), 10 April, p. 2, viewed 9 July 2019, http://nla.gov.au/nla.news-article88229711

10. 1874 'THE LADIES' CRICKET MATCH', *Melbourne Punch* (Vic.: 1855–1900), 9 April, p. 8, viewed 7 Nov 2019, http://nla.gov.au/nla.news-article174547478

11. 1874 'WOMAN!', *The Herald* (Melbourne, Vic.: 1861–1954), 11 April, p. 2, viewed 7 Nov 2019, http://nla.gov.au/nla.news-article245309186
12. 1874 'No Title', *The Maryborough and Dunolly Advertiser*, 13 April 1874, Victorian State Library microfilm.
13. 1874 'RAE', *The Herald* (Melbourne, Vic.: 1861–1954), 16 April, p. 2, viewed 7 Nov 2019, http://nla.gov.au/nla.news-article245309328
14. 1874 'No Title', *The Maryborough and Dunolly Advertiser*, 20 April 1874, Victorian State Library microfilm.
15. 1874 'No Titlev *The Ballarat Courier* (Vic.: 1869–1883; 1914–1918), 25 April, p. 2, viewed 7 Nov 2019, http://nla.gov.au/nla.news-article192282125; 1874 'No Title', *The Herald* (Melbourne, Vic.: 1861–1954), 25 April, p. 2, viewed 7 Nov 2019, http://nla.gov.au/nla.news-article245306076
16. 1874 'A LADIES CRICKET MATCH AT STEIGLITZ', *Geelong Advertiser* (Vic.: 1859–1929), 27 May, p. 3, viewed 9 Nov 2019, http://nla.gov.au/nla.news-article147368767
17. 1874 'TOWN TALK', *Geelong Advertiser* (Vic.: 1859–1929), 27 May, p. 2, viewed 7 Nov 2019, http://nla.gov.au/nla.news-article147368784
18. 1874 'NEW SOUTH WALES CRICKET ASSOCIATION', *Australian Town and Country Journal* (Sydney, NSW: 1870–1907), 24 October, p. 31, viewed 7 Nov 2019, http://nla.gov.au/nla.news-article70485870
19. 1874 British Newspaper Archive, *Edinburgh Evening News*, 9 June 1874, p. 4, viewed 5 Nov 2019, https://www.british newspaperarchive.co.uk/viewer/bl/0000452/18740609/067/0004
20. 1874 *New Orleans Republican*. [volume] (New Orleans, La), 4 July 1874, Chronicling America: Historic American Newspapers. Lib. of Congress, viewed 5 Nov 2019, https://chroniclingamerica.loc.gov/lccn/sn83016555/1874-07-04/ed-1/seq-2/; 1874 *Public Ledger*. [volume] (Memphis, Tenn.), 19 Sept. 1874, Chronicling America: Historic American Newspapers. Lib. of Congress, viewed 5 Nov 2019, https://chroniclingamerica.loc.gov/lccn/sn85033673/1874-09-19/ed-1/seq-1/

21. 1874 British Newspaper Archive, *Buckingham Advertiser and Free Press*, 15 August 1874, p.1, Viewed 5 Nov 2019, [subscriber content] https://www.britishnewspaperarchive.co.uk/viewer/bl/0001081/18740815/028/0001
22. 1874 'CRICKET IN ENGLAND', *The Sydney Mail and New South Wales Advertiser* (NSW: 1871–1912), 17 October, p. 495, viewed 7 Nov 2019, http://nla.gov.au/nla.news-article162482215
23. 1875 'THE EASTER FAIR', *Bendigo Advertiser* (Vic.: 1855–1918), 30 March, p. 2, viewed 24 Feb 2021, http://nla.gov.au/nla.news-article88257785
24. 1875 'THE EASTER FAIR', *Bendigo Advertiser* (Vic.: 1855–1918), 1 April, p. 2, viewed 5 Nov 2019, http://nla.gov.au/nla.news-article88257841
25. 1875 'THE LADIES' CRICKET MATCH AT SANDHURST', *The Age* (Melbourne, Vic.: 1854–1954), 1 April, p. 3, viewed 5 Nov 2019, http://nla.gov.au/nla.newsarticle202136770
26. 1875 'THE LADIES' CRICKET MATCH', *Bendigo Advertiser* (Vic.: 1855–1918), 3 April, p. 3, viewed 5 Nov 2019, http://nla.gov.au/nla.news-article88257919
27. 1875 'THE LADIES' CRICKET MATCH AT SANDHURST', *The Age* (Melbourne, Vic.: 1854–1954), 1 April, p. 3, viewed 5 Nov 2019, http://nla.gov.au/nla.news-article202136770
28. 1875 'COMMERCIAL', *The Age* (Melbourne, Vic.: 1854–1954), 1 April, p. 2, viewed 5 Nov 2019, http://nla.gov.au/nla.news-article202136793
29. 1875 'LADY CRICKETERS', *The Herald* (Melbourne, Vic.: 1861–1954), 1 April, p. 2, viewed 5 Nov 2019, http://nla.gov.au/nla.news-article244178712
30. 1875 'LADY CRICKETERS', *The Herald* (Melbourne, Vic.:1861–1954), 1 April, p. 2, viewed 5 Nov 2019, http://nla.gov.au/nla.news-article244178712
31. 1875 'The Argus', *The Argus* (Melbourne, Vic.: 1848–1957), 7 April, p. 7, viewed 7 Nov 2019, http://nla.gov.au/nla.news-article11514859
32. 1875 'CRICKET GOSSIP', *Leader* (Melbourne, Vic.: 1862–1918, 1935), 10 April, p. 11, viewed 5 Nov 2019, http://nla.gov.au/nla.news-article197936475

33. 1875 'THE BENDIGO ADVERTISER', *Bendigo Advertiser* (Vic.: 1855–1918), 15 April, p. 2, viewed 7 Nov 2019, http://nla.gov.au/nla.news-article88258308
34. 1875 'NEWS AND NOTES', *The Ballarat Star* (Vic.: 1865–1924), 17 April, p. 2, viewed 7 Nov 2019, http://nla.gov.au/nla.news-article208253128
35. 1875 'SPORTING NOTES', *The Age* (Melbourne, Vic.: 1854–1954), 19 April, p. 3, viewed 7 Nov 2019, http://nla.gov.au/nla.news-article202134738
36. 1875 'TOWN TALK', *Geelong Advertiser* (Vic.: 1859–1929), 26 April, p. 2, viewed 10 July 2019, http://nla.gov.au/nla.news-article148775550
37. 1886 'The Ladies' Cricket Match', *Illustrated Sydney News* (NSW: 1881–1894), 15 May, p. 3, viewed 19 Feb 2021, http://nla.gov.au/nla.news-article63620112
38. 1889 'SOCIAL NOTES', *The Australasian* (Melbourne, Vic.: 1864–1946), 9 November, p. 42, viewed 5 Nov 2019, http://nla.gov.au/nla.news-article139137865; 1888 'THE PICTORIAL', *The Australasian* (Melbourne, Vic.: 1864–1946), 1 December, p. 11, viewed 5 Nov 2019, http://nla.gov.au/nla.news-article142433314
39. 1888 'SOCIETY AND FASHION', *The Australasian* (Melbourne, Vic.: 1864–1946), 24 November, p. 50, viewed 24 Feb 2021, http://nla.gov.au/nla.news-article142433004
40. 1890 'LADY CRICKETERS IN ENGLAND', *The Age* (Melbourne, Vic.: 1854–1954), 29 September, p. 5, viewed 7 Nov 2019, http://nla.gov.au/nla.news-article196983294
41. 1890 'LADIES CRICKET CLUB', *The Herald* (Melbourne, Vic.: 1861–1954), 7 October, p. 4, viewed 7 Nov 2019, http://nla.gov.au/nla.news-article242110231; 1890 'A LADIES' CRICKET CLUB', *The Herald* (Melbourne, Vic.: 1861–1954), 18 December, p. 4, viewed 7 Nov 2019, http://nla.gov.au/nla.news-article242107821; 1890 'CORRESPONDENCE', *Sportsman* (Melbourne, Vic.: 1882–1904), 1 October, p. 6, viewed 7 Nov 2019, http://nla.gov.au/nla.news-article227934656
42. 1890 'LADIES' CRICKET', *The Herald* (Melbourne, Vic.: 1861–1954), 11 November, p. 3, viewed 7 Nov 2019, http://nla.gov.au/nla.news-article242104489

43. 1890 'TELEGRAMS', *The Hay Standard and Advertiser for Balranald, Wentworth, Maude…* (Hay, NSW: 1871–1873; 1880–1881; 1890–1900), 31 December, p. 3, viewed 19 Feb 2021, http://nla.gov.au/nla.news-article144685428

44. 1891 'LADIES' CRICKET MATCH AT SYDNEY', *The Age* (Melbourne, Vic.: 1854–1954), 18 March, p. 7, viewed 7 Nov 2019, http://nla.gov.au/nla.news-article201459347

45. 1895 'LADIES' CRICKET MATCH', *The Kyneton Observer* (Vic.: 1856–1900), 16 March, p. 4, viewed 7 Nov 2019, http://nla.gov.au/nla.news-article240956652

46. Births, deaths and marriages, family history search, viewed 18 Oct 2019, https://my.rio.bdm.vic.gov.au/efamily-history/5da805127ffbba63c698f2fd/results?q=efamily

47. 1884 'FAMILY NOTICES', *Bendigo Advertiser* (Vic.: 1855–1918), 3 May, p. 2, viewed 7 Nov 2019, http://nla.gov.au/nla.news-article88998911

48. 1894 'DEATH OF MR. JOHN RAE', *The Bendigo Independent* (Vic.: 1891–1918), 17 July, p. 2, viewed 24 Feb 2021, http://nla.gov.au/nla.news-article183314961

49. 1883 'THE BENDIGO ADVERTISER', *Bendigo Advertiser* (Vic.: 1855–1918), 2 August, p. 2, viewed 7 Nov 2019, http://nla.gov.au/nla.news-article88518829; 1883 'Family Notices', *North Melbourne Advertiser* (Vic.: 1873–1894), 7 September, p. 2, viewed 7 Nov 2019, http://nla.gov.au/nla.news-article66159473

50. 1952 'Family Notices', *The Argus* (Melbourne, Vic.: 1848–1957), 8 November, p. 16, viewed 7 Nov 2019, http://nla.gov.au/nla.news-article23212349

51. Greensborough Historical Society, *World War I Project 2015–2017*, 'Edward Rae Cordner', viewed 7 Nov 2019, https://victoriancollections.net.au/media/collectors/4f729f5697f83e03086015b8/items/5938c06cd0cdd41fdc6818b4/item-media/5a7418c421ea790474abb6de/original.docx

52. 1887 'CRICKET FOR LADIES', *The Australasian* (Melbourne, Vic.: 1864–1946), 29 January, p. 7, viewed 7 Nov 2019, http://nla.gov.au/nla.news-article142176044

www.ingramcontent.com/pod-product-compliance
Lightning Source LLC
Chambersburg PA
CBHW022020290426
44109CB00015B/1247